HELLO SUMMER
Cut, Glue & Other Activities

www.mamaishere.com

"We must find time to stop and thank the people who make a difference in our lives."
- John F. Kennedy

So, I would like to say: THANK YOU!

Hi! I used to be a nanny when I was a teenager, then a tutor and a teacher (at the same time I got my Bachelor's Degree in Design) . Nowadays, I am a designer and a mom - or how I like to call it: mama). This is how "Mama Is Here" was born!

I hope I am making a difference in your children's lives and thank you for making one in mine!

@mamaishere2021

follow to check daily activities you can do with your little one!

For FREE learning video resources, subscribe to my channel:

You Tube bit.ly/Mamaishere

Dear Teachers & Parents,

It is recommended that you are an active part of the learning process: help your child learn, count the objects with them, praise their improvement, etc. Also avoid long sessions and try working on lessons when the kid is not feeling tired.

I hope I'm providing your kid the ability to count, spell, and develop many other skills as they play the summer games!

Thank you again and have fun!

Cheers,
Kelle Lima

Check out other books from "Little Fingers" collection, such as:

TRACING LETTERS:
ASL Handwriting Book

Set up!

1. The "Summer Time!" page will be the "board of your activity". Don't cut it!

2. Cut the clothes below and in the following pages into individual pieces using the dotted lines as a guide

How to play!

The child should grab different clothing pieces and dress the kids as they wish, let their creativity speak for them! **Play with a Twist**: Ask your child to get a specific color, or item. This will increase their vocabulary, learn colors, etc. You can also ask the child to get an item for a body part, teaching them each part. You can either store pieces in a ziploc bag or envelope (templates at the end of the book) to replay OR glue different sets in each "Get Ready!" page.

This page is blank because you will cut pieces print on the other side. Follow us on Instagram for activity ideas: @mamaishere2021

Summer Dress Up: Cut Pieces Below

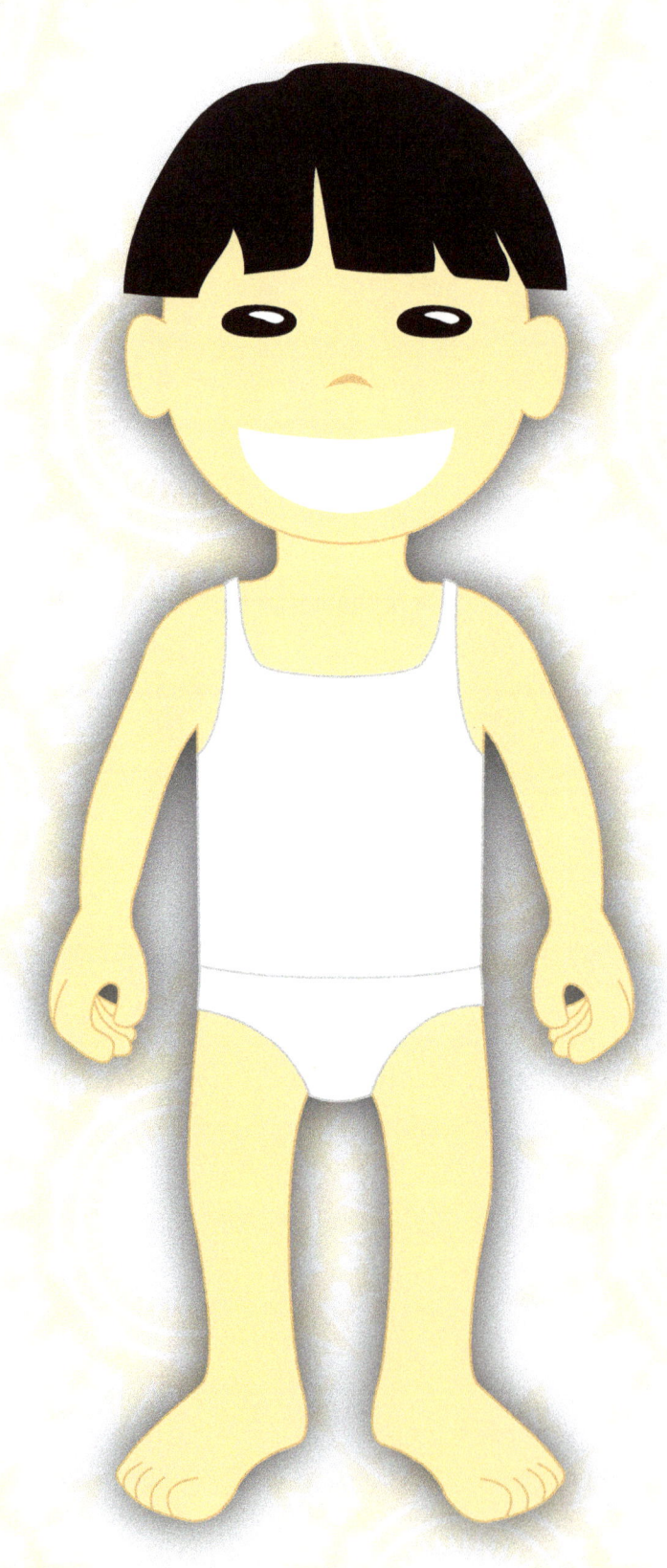

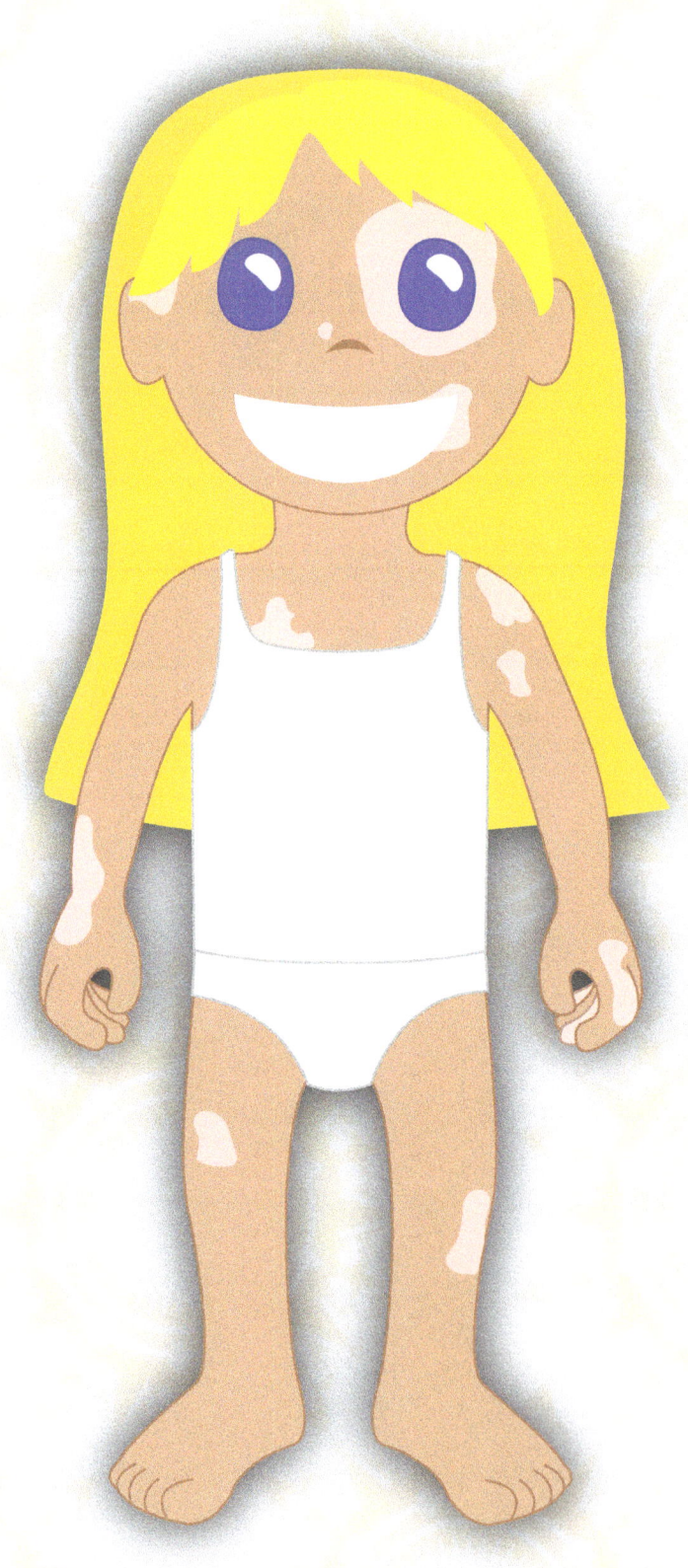

Summer Beach Activity! (Instructions)

Set up!
1. The "Crabby Shelly Beach!" page will be the "board of your game". Don't cut it
2. Cut crabs, shells, numbers, and shape bases into individual pieces

How to play!
Play 1: Add a blue circle on the top of the board. They will dictate a number and object type (e.g.: "white 2" = "2 shells", "red 3" = "3 crabs"). The child should add the number of objects requested to the sand side. **Play with a Twist:** Add the items yourself and ask your child to grab the numbers, teach addition, or pretend play.
Play 2: place objects to create different shapes by using the shapes boards.

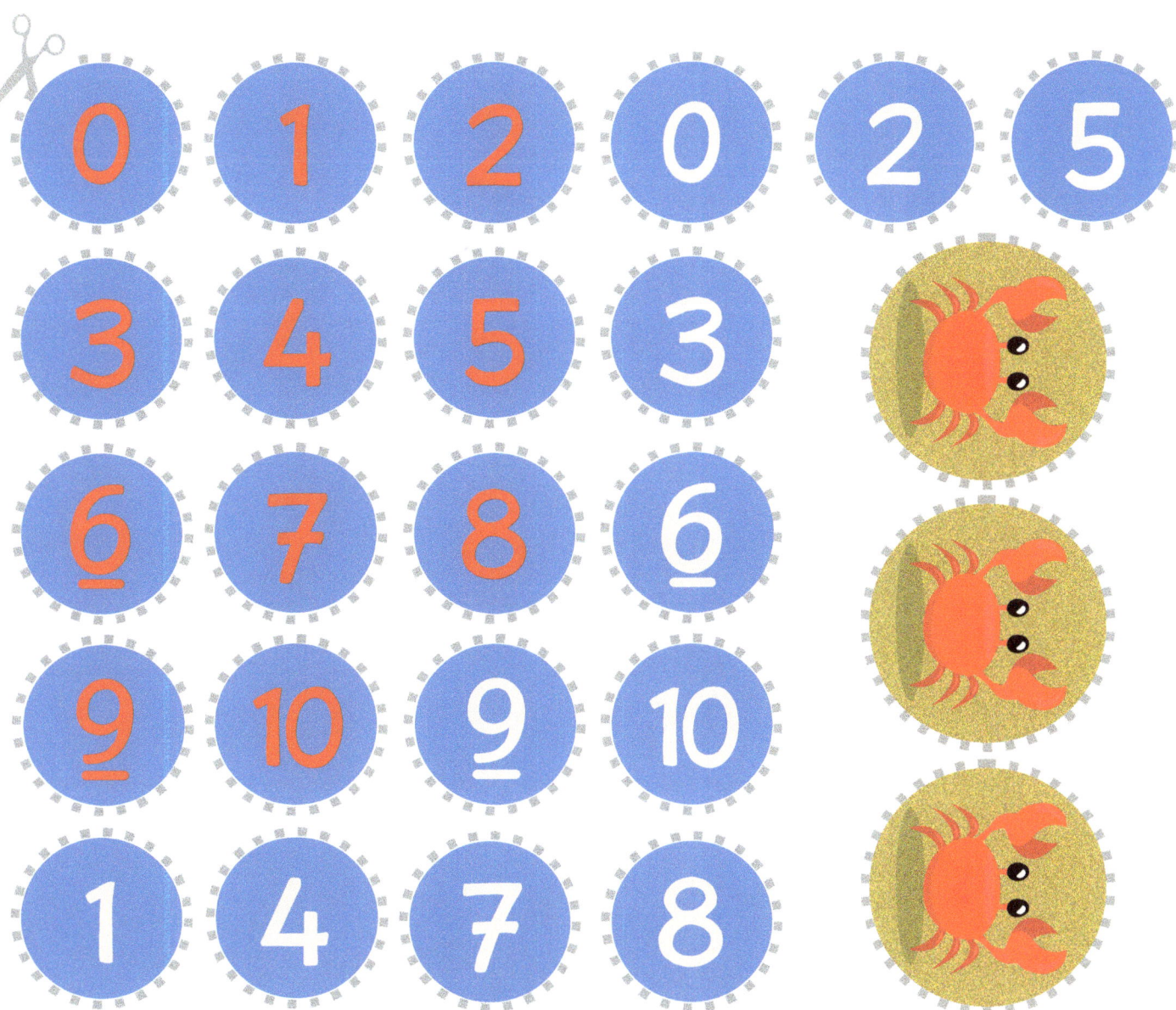

This page is blank because you will cut pieces print on the other side. Follow us on Instagram for activity ideas: @mamaishere2021

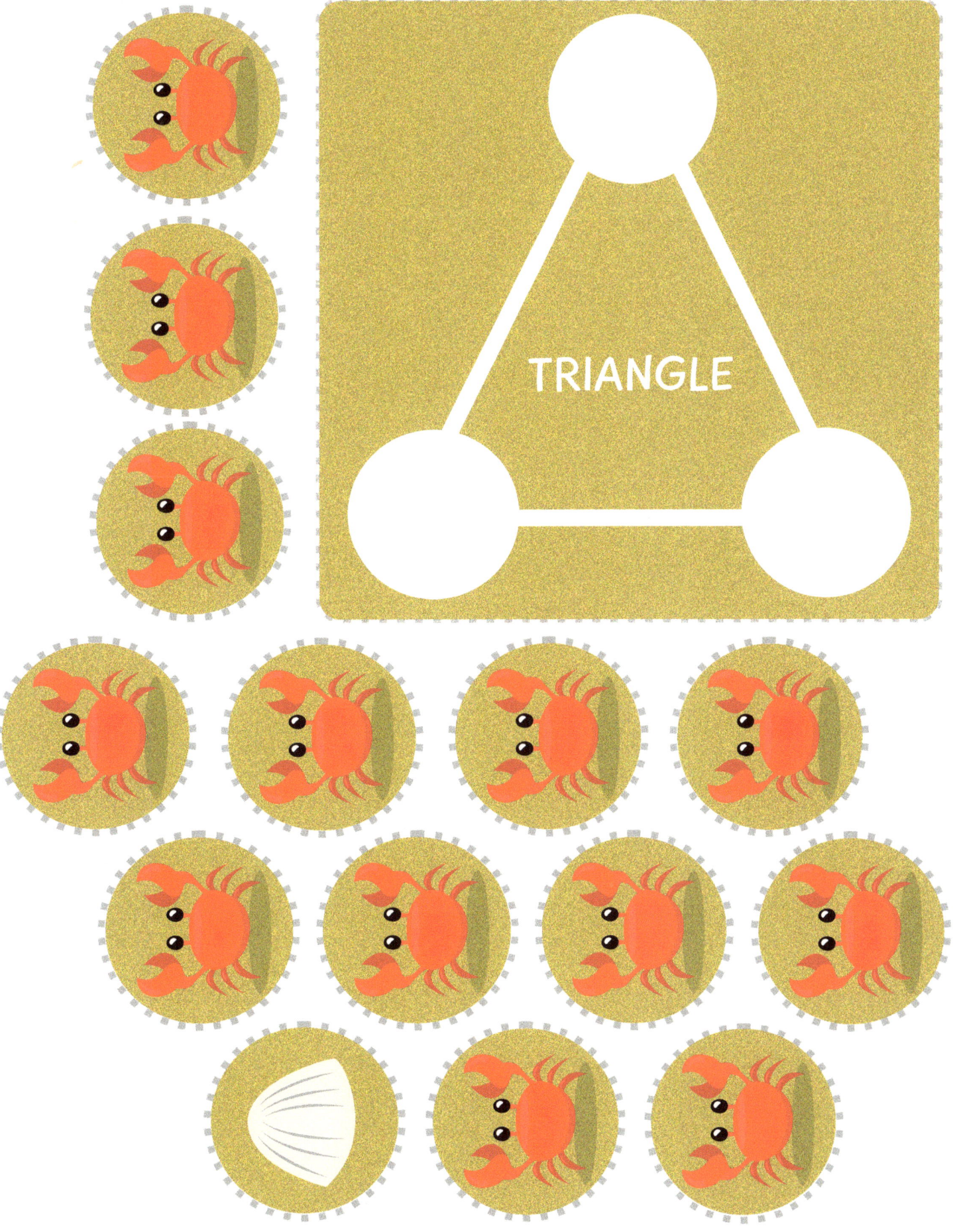

This page is blank because you will cut pieces print on the other side. Check other products at mamaishere.com

This page is blank because you will cut pieces print on the other side. Follow us on Instagram for activity ideas: @mamaishere2021

 This page is blank because you will cut pieces print on the other side. Check other products at mamaishere.com

I Spy! (Instructions)

Set up!
1. "I Spy: Summer Vacation!" (previous) page will be the "game's board". Don't cut it
2. Cut the objects below into individual pieces
3. Store pieces in a ziploc bag or envelope (model on last page) for future play

How to play!
Add random amounts of objects and add a copy to the bottom. Ask the child to count and put the respective number above it! **Play with a Twist**: Ask your child to get a specific item, items of a specific color, colors, etc. You can also add the numbers and ask the child to add the objects, or them check if you add the correct numbers, etc.

This page is blank because you will cut pieces print on the other side. Follow us on Instagram for activity ideas: @mamaishere2021

Shadow Game!

Cut pieces below to play match face up for younger kids, and face down for older ones.

Set up!
1. Cut the colored watermelon slices into individual pieces

How to play!
Mix all pieces with the print facing up. Then teach your child to match the amount of seeds to their respective number (or the bonus matching shapes)! **Play with a Twist:** For older kids, face all pieces down and take turns with your child while playing a matching memory game! You can also combine different pieces in an entire watermelon to teach addition, etc. When ready, glue them to their slots on the line work (or store them in an envelpe).

This page is blank because you will cut pieces print on the other side. Follow us on Instagram for activity ideas: @mamaishere2021

 This page is blank because you will cut pieces print on the other side. Check other products at mamaishere.com

Watermelon Matching!

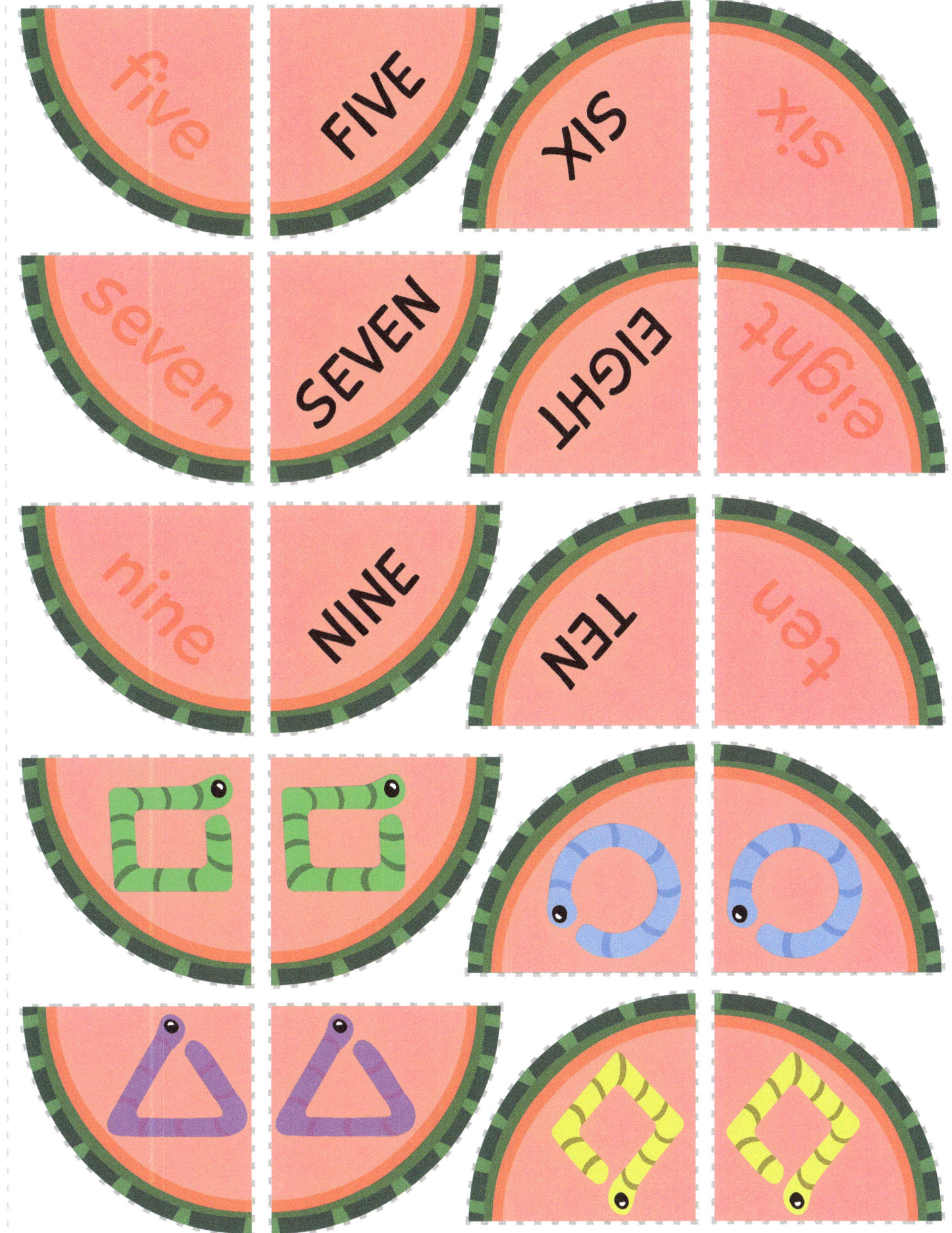

This page is blank because you will cut pieces print on the other side. Follow us on Instagram for activity ideas: @mamaishere2021

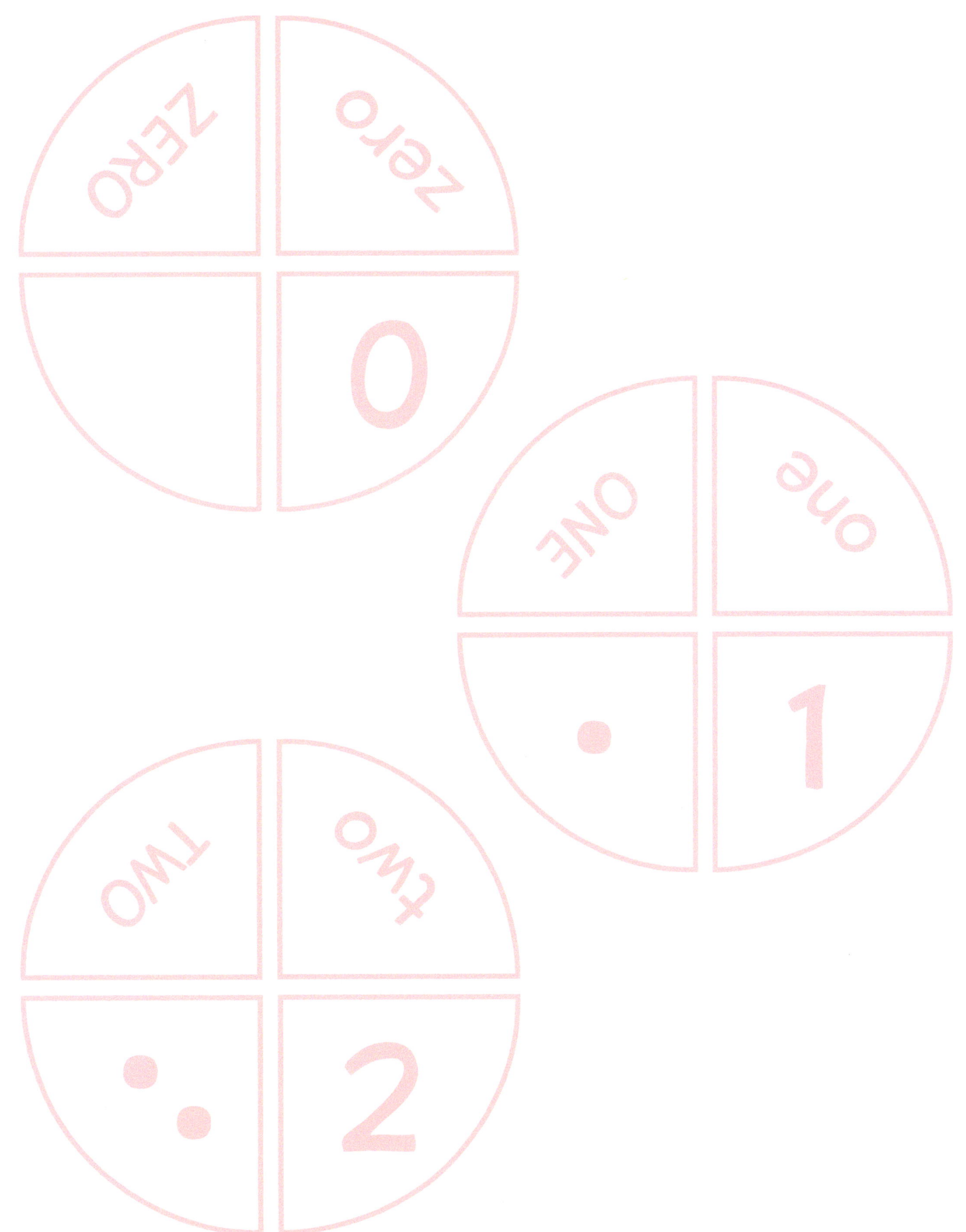

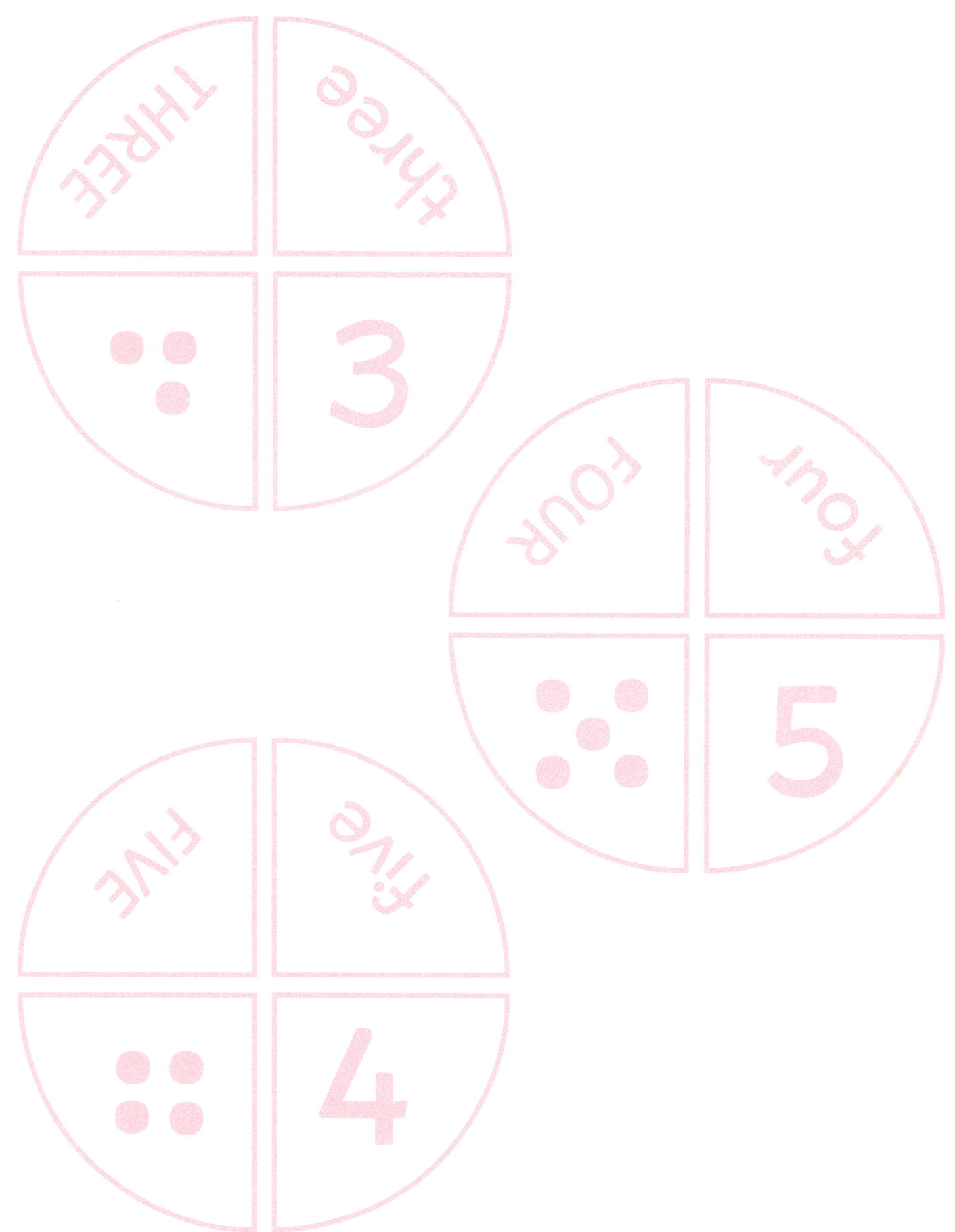

Sliced Watermellon Puzzle

Set up!

1. Cut the objects below into individual pieces
2. The "Pineapple Puzzle!" page will be the "board of your game". Don't cut it

How to play!

Let your child add each lump into its slot on the pineapple. Then mix all pieces with the print facing up and either let your kid do each letter on their desired order, or ask them to find and glue a specific letter to glue in the word slot thei belong to.

Play with a Twist: count as you add the lumps, create different combinations using the available letters from the word pineapple (e.g: N + A + P: nap!) or use them to go over phonics.

Pineapple Puzzle!

Beach Dots (Instructions)

Set up!
1. Cut the circles below into individual pieces
2. The "Beach Dots!!" (previous) page will be the "board of your game". Don't cut it

How to play!
Mix all pieces with the print facing upwards.

Play with your child to fit each circle to its spot matching the surrounding colors. Some pieces are easier (one color) or harder (needs to be adjusted to match more than one color, lines, etc.)

Go little by little so that your child can learn!

Play with a Twist: tell your child to get a circle of a specific color, count how many pieces are left, etc.

 This page is blank because you will cut pieces print on the other side. Follow us on Instagram for activity ideas: @mamaishere2021

Set up!

1. Cut the circles below into individual pieces
2. The "Beach Dots!!" (previous) page will be the "board of your game". Don't cut it

How to play!

Mix all pieces with the print facing upwards.

Play with your child to fit each circle to its spot matching the surrounding colors. Some pieces are easier (one color) or harder (needs to be adjusted to match more than one color, lines, etc.)

Go little by little so that your child can learn!

Play with a Twist: tell your child to get a circle of a specific color, count how many pieces are left, etc.

 This page is blank because you will cut pieces print on the other side. Follow us on Instagram for activity ideas: @mamaishere2021

Beach Scavenger Hunt!

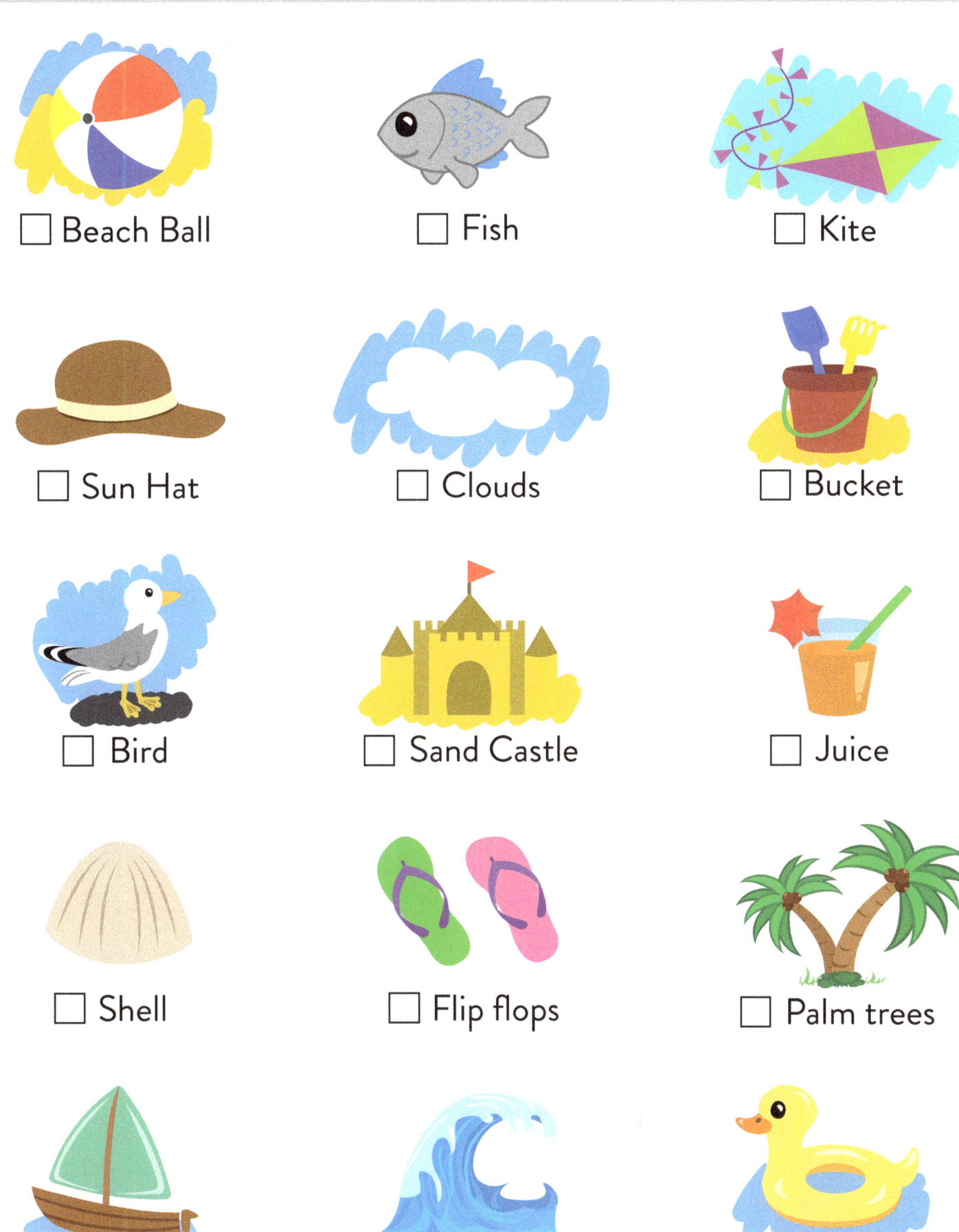

- ☐ Beach Ball
- ☐ Fish
- ☐ Kite
- ☐ Sun Hat
- ☐ Clouds
- ☐ Bucket
- ☐ Bird
- ☐ Sand Castle
- ☐ Juice
- ☐ Shell
- ☐ Flip flops
- ☐ Palm trees
- ☐ Boat
- ☐ Waves
- ☐ Float

Set up!

1. Cut the sandles below into individual pieces
2. The "Lost Sandles: Time To Match!" (previous) page will be the "board of your game". Don't cut it

How to play!

Mix all pieces with the print facing upwards.

Play with your child to match each pair of sandles to its respective owner!

Play with a Twist: face all pieces down and play a memory game to then glue the sandles on their respective slots.

This page is blank because you will cut pieces print on the other side. Check other products at mamaishere.com

Over
Tab

Cut _____
Fold _ _ _ _
Glue ⊠

HERE
mama is
⊠

⊠

⊠

Glue on the inner part

Glue on the inner part

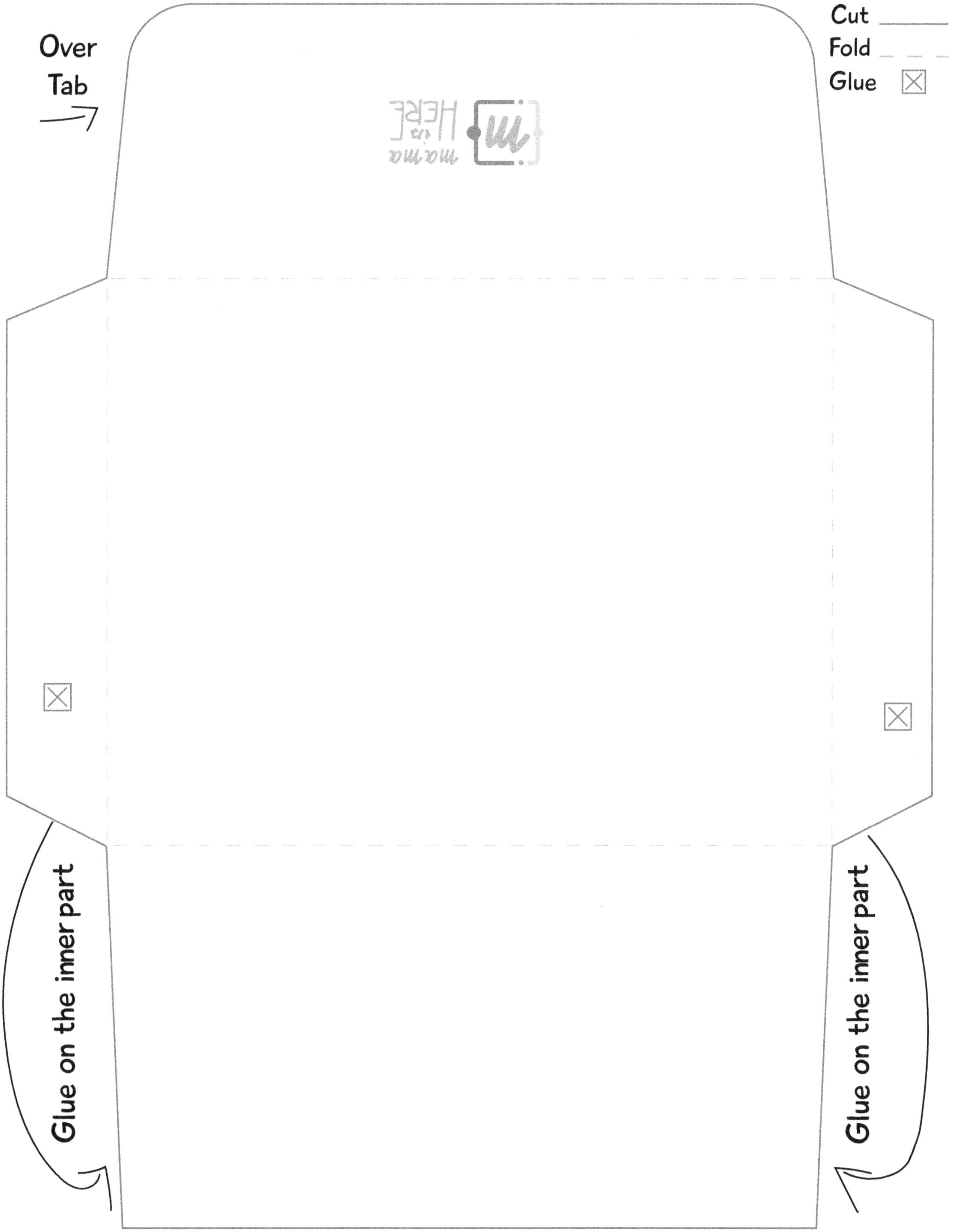

This page is blank because you will cut pieces print on the other side. Follow us on Instagram for activity ideas: @mamaishere2021

Traditional Envelope Template!

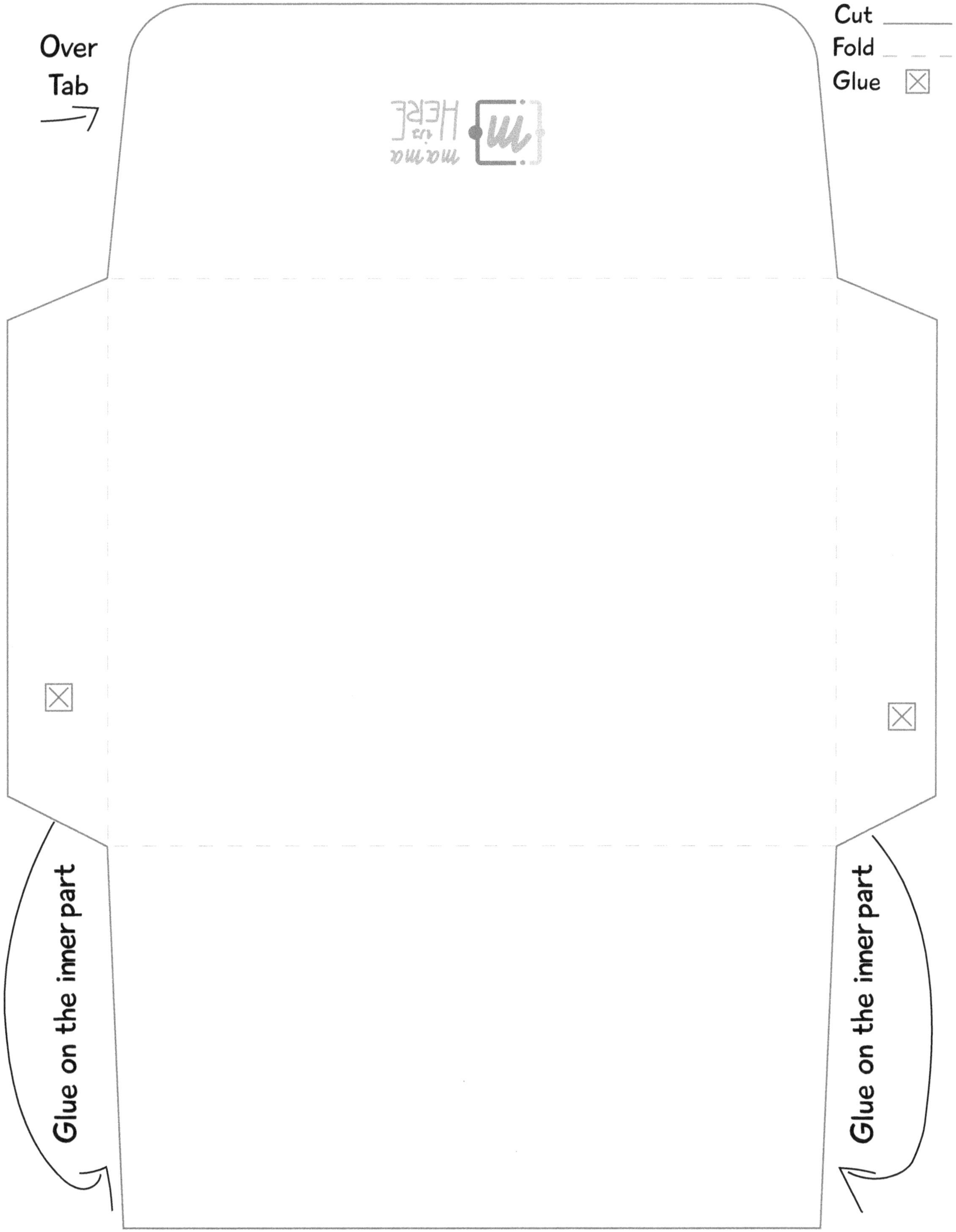

Cut _____
Fold _ _ _ _
Glue ⊠

Over
Tab

mama HERE

⊠

⊠

Glue on the inner part

Glue on the inner part

Traditional Envelope Template!

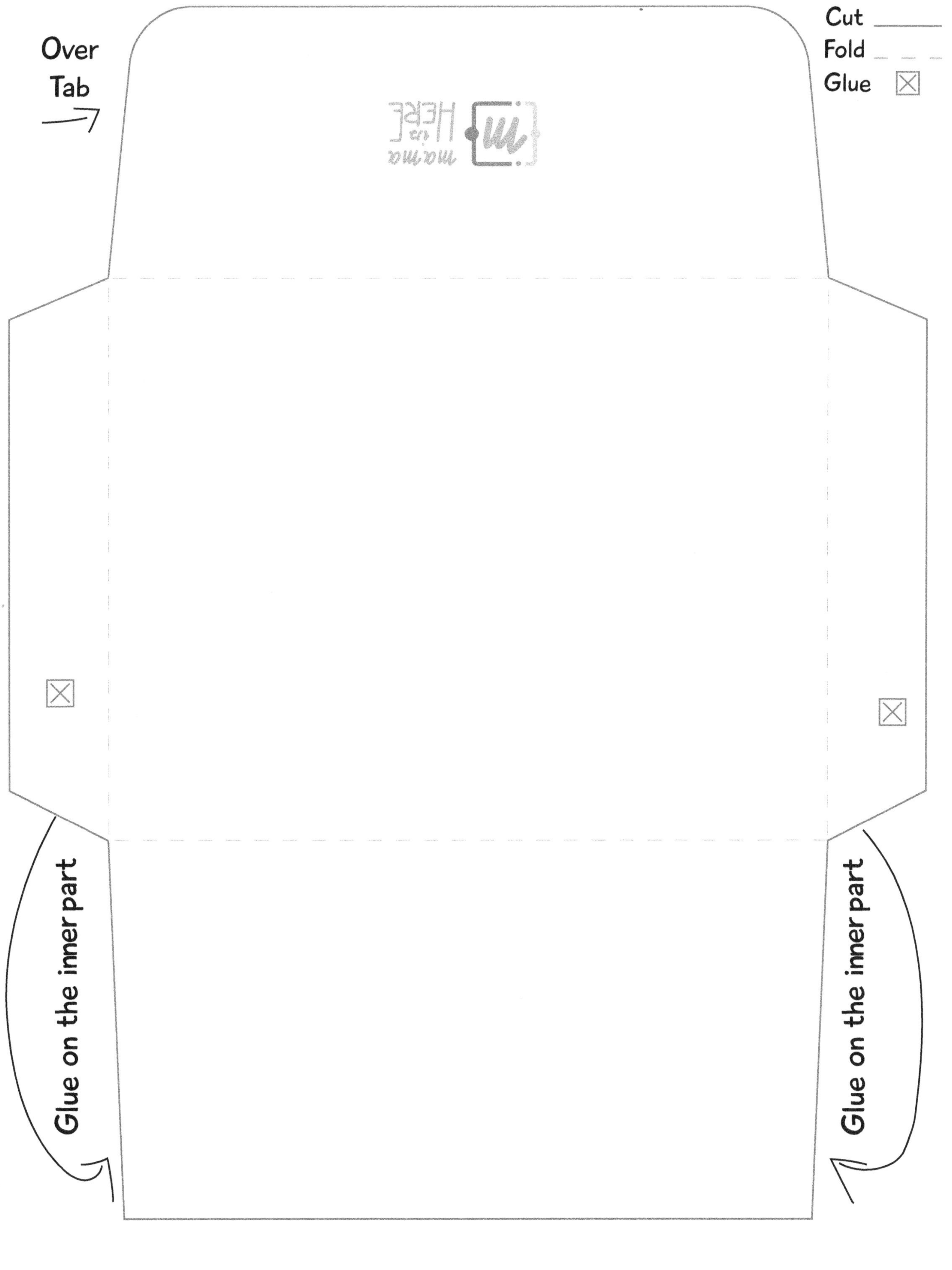

Cut _____
Fold - - - -
Glue ⊠

Over
Tab

CUT HERE
mama

⊠

⊠

Glue on the inner part

Glue on the inner part

 This page is blank because you will cut pieces print on the other side. Follow us on Instagram for activity ideas: @mamaishere2021

Traditional Envelope Template!

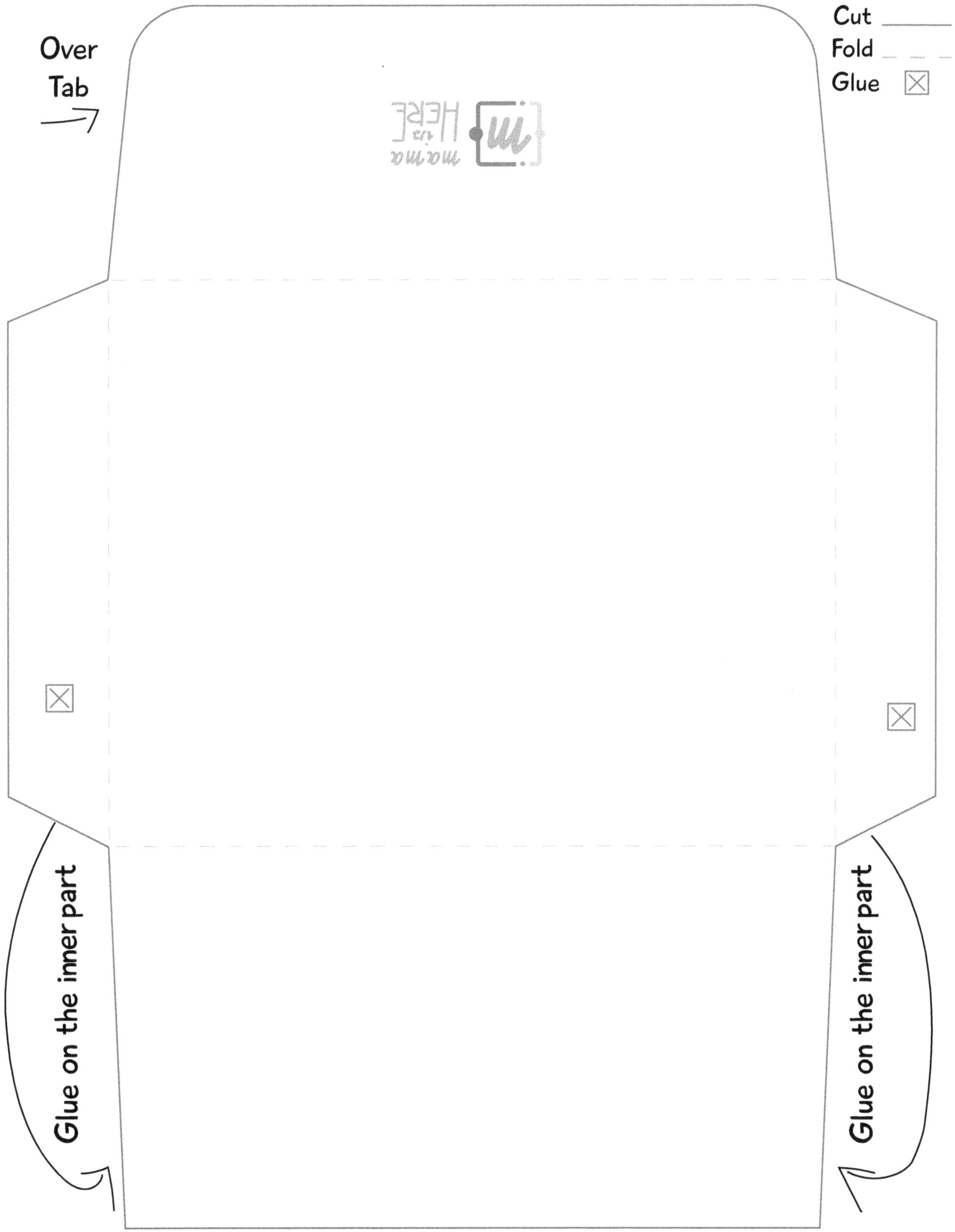

Cut _____
Fold _ _ _ _
Glue ⊠

Over
Tab →

mama HERE
ⓜ

⊠

⊠

Glue on the inner part

Glue on the inner part

This page is blank because you will cut pieces print on the other side. Check other products at mamaishere.com

Check some of my other books at:
www.amazon.com/author/kellelima

Scan this code with your phone!

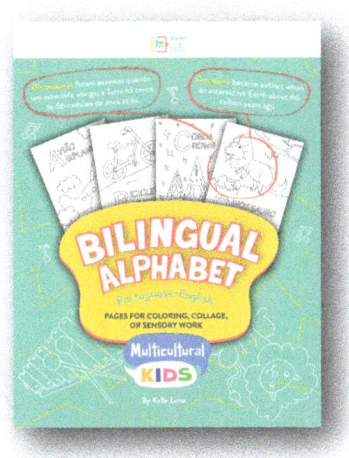

Hi there, I hope your learning journey has been great!

Did you enjoy this book?
Please consider leaving a
positive review!

I would love to connect with you:

  @mamaishere2021

www.ingramcontent.com/pod-product-compliance
Lightning Source LLC
Chambersburg PA
CBHW040512150626
46551CB00030B/2524